Things University Doesn't Teach You

SARAH ADENAIKE

authorHOUSE®

AuthorHouse™ UK
1663 Liberty Drive
Bloomington, IN 47403 USA
www.authorhouse.co.uk
Phone: 0800.197.4150

© 2018 Sarah Adenaike. All rights reserved.

No part of this book may be reproduced, stored in a retrieval system, or transmitted by any means without the written permission of the author.

Published by AuthorHouse 02/09/2017

ISBN: 978-1-5462-8422-2 (sc)
ISBN: 978-1-5462-8423-9 (hc)
ISBN: 978-1-5462-8663-9 (e)

Print information available on the last page.

Any people depicted in stock imagery provided by Thinkstock are models, and such images are being used for illustrative purposes only.
Certain stock imagery © Thinkstock.

This book is printed on acid-free paper.

Because of the dynamic nature of the Internet, any web addresses or links contained in this book may have changed since publication and may no longer be valid. The views expressed in this work are solely those of the author and do not necessarily reflect the views of the publisher, and the publisher hereby disclaims any responsibility for them.

CONTENTS

Acknowledgements vii

The What and the Why 1
My Story 3
Let's Begin 6
Mentorship and Why It Matters 10
The Importance of Networking 14
Manage Your Finances, or They Will Manage You 17
Time Out 21
Walk the Walk, Don't Just Talk the Talk 24
The Importance of Self-Esteem 27
Time: Our Most Precious Gift 31
Goals and Deadlines 33
A Degree Alone Does Not Equal a Job or a Better Future 36
Get Involved in Extracurricular Activities 40
Practice Thinking Outside the Box 42
Your Curriculum Vitae (CV) 44
Self-Development 48
Factors to Consider When Job Hunting 50
Gaining Work Experience 53
Persistence Is Crucial 58
The Future Is Yours 62

Useful Resources 67
About the Author 69

ACKNOWLEDGEMENTS

This book has passed through several hands, too numerous to mention, but I consider my appreciation a disservice if I fail to mention just a few.

Primarily, I thank God Almighty for the conceptualisation, motivation, and courage to get started despite mitigating circumstances.

My well of gratitude goes to my wonderful family and close friends for their understanding and unrelenting support, most especially, my son, Joseph, for missing out on mom–son time.

I'm also grateful to editor Kate McCarthy, all the way from South Africa, for her input and "eagle-eyeing" every detail.

While thanking all, I accept full responsibility for any inadequacy that may inadvertently creep into this book.

Testimonials

Sarah Adenaike's keen voice has the authenticity and observation borne of extensive experience in compliance. She knows her subject and shares the secrets you need to succeed in the work place. Whether you're in your first job, a student seeking employment, or a long-time professional, Sarah's rules of the road will help you meet your goals. She communicates in a straightforward way that makes this first-class read easily digestible and insightful. I wish I had read it years ago.

—Lisa Kate Osofsky, EMEA Regional Chair of Exiger, LLC, and former MLRO at GSI

Inspiring, thought-provoking, and allusive. It is a must read for young people in education, apprenticeship, and others in need of new career path or inspiration to take that bold next step. Whilst this book would shape many careers and ideas, vision2mission, under whose content the book was written, intends to provide further resource via an application launching soon, that would further help actualise an individual's goals and aspirations. Be on the lookout!

—Olu Koya, Consultant

You should be proud! Your words ring in my ears, and I am actively following your advice! You made an impression on your first reader.

—Kate McCarthy, editor

She arrived with a black travel case full of papers and laptops, and carried a smile of humble self-awareness. We talked about work and life; she raised her palm in what I thought was a high five when the topic of child care came up. But instead, she clasped her hand around mine and laughed in recognition of the difficulties of working mothers. This is how I met Sarah, on the thirty-second floor of a building in London's Canary Wharf, and this was what hinted at her amazing sincerity.

This book that Sarah went on to write distils that sincerity in anecdotes and experiences a formal education cannot hope to provide. As Sir Ken Robinson, a leading authority on modern education, explains in his literature, more people are now armed with university degrees than in previous decades; bachelor's, master's, PhDs, MBAs, the list goes on. But what sets one aside from others in such a competitive environment? The reality is we leave formal education with a piece of paper that certifies us as being "qualified," but having learnt the hard way, what colleagues, employers, and partners—in business and life—value more is experience. Do you remember that 1990's television series *Doogie Howser, M.D.*? A fourteen-year-old surgeon with no experience would be difficult to trust, even if I was shown his medical degree from Princeton.

> Experience is greatest gift you can give yourself. Push through those difficult jobs and bosses; give yourself relationships and travel; allow yourself pain, sorrow, happiness; meet your problems head on. I hope this book helps plant the seed of self-investment. But it will be up to the reader to water that seed and reap the rewards.
>
> **—Anonymous**

As an undergraduate student, Sarah was a student representative for Law, an ambassador for Law, a member of the Staff-Student Liaison Committee and an active member of the Students' Union. Generous with her time and experience as an undergraduate, it is no surprise that Sarah has used her time and experience as a graduate to collate and articulate such wonderful hints, tips and advice to benefit others.

As Sarah explains, creating the future you desire requires more than a degree. While many students balance paid (or voluntary) work with their study commitments, and all students graduate with a range of skills and abilities that make them employable, it is how you use your skills and abilities, how you learn from your experience and the experience of others, that really makes a difference. With advice on everything from networking and mentorship to self-development and creating your own opportunities, this guide is informative, reassuring, and a 'must have' for anyone preparing for the world of work. Good luck!

Penny Brearey-Horne
Senior Lecturer in Law,
The School of Law and the Human Rights Centre.
Student Conduct Officer,
The University of Essex

**Should
Would
Could
Did**

THE WHAT AND THE WHY

A university degree is undoubtedly an invaluable asset, but there are aspects to the real world that no university is equipped to teach. These are the life lessons only those who have walked the path are able to share. As one of those who have indeed walked the path, I have tried to capture the essence and challenges of the real world that awaits us once the structured days of university or college lectures are over.

The purpose of this book is to sum up, clearly and succinctly, the lessons I learned over a decade; lessons that many undergraduates and graduates need to learn if they are to succeed in today's fast-paced and highly competitive global marketplace.

> Many university students do not fully understand the world beyond university. I believe this book will help them by providing some insights along the way. Likewise, there are graduates out there who are still trying to "figure things out," and I believe this book will also benefit them.

I like to think that I can save the reader years of slow discovery by providing a snapshot of what you need to know post-university or college. Here is my personal treasure trove of tips and advice that explains in detail how the real world works and how to not just succeed but to thrive amid the challenges.

What is your vision and how will you make it your mission.

MY STORY

Once I completed my degree, I felt fully equipped to face the real world. I was excited to start exploring the opportunities that awaited me. But I soon discovered my expectations were unrealistic.

Prior to embarking on my workplace journey, I genuinely believed that as a law graduate, I would be able to pick and choose jobs as I desired. I expected to be in high demand; after all, the degree prospectus had suggested as much. But alas, I quickly discovered competition for available openings was stiff.

> **Over time, I realised there are many things we do not learn in class. University can teach us so much but fails to teach us about the challenges that can impact our day-to-day lives post-graduation.**

So, the inspiration for this book began, and I made a commitment to share my experiences with would-be graduates, graduates, and others to ensure they are more fully equipped for the real deal.

This book focuses on what I learnt during my personal journey. These lessons did not form part of my academic or social life at university, but they formed a vital part of life after academic pursuits.

My hope is that this book will have a positive impact on your life and add value to it. If it does, that is my reward. Nothing excites me more than adding value to the lives of others. For the curious reader, my vision is to reach and empower at least a million lives. This vision has now become my mission.

I dare ask, what is your vision, and how will you make it your mission?

In addition to reading and acquiring knowledge, it is very important to ask ourselves thought- provoking questions from time to time.

Questions :

- What are your goals?
- How can you achieve them?
- What inspires you?
- What does success mean to you?
- If you were not afraid, what would you do differently?
- What are your limitations?
- What are you doing about them?
- What are you doing daily to improve yourself?
- Do your friends add value to you?
- Are you investing in yourself?
- What are your long-term plans?
- What do you want to be remembered for?
- Why don't you take action NOW ?

Base your decisions on where you going, not where you are.

LET'S BEGIN

Even before I began my tertiary education, I decided I would find my niche in top-tier organisations. My assumption was, quite simply, that I would graduate with a top degree and then take my place in the elite world I envisaged. Little did I realise then that my degree was just the beginning of this journey. I now understand that learning is a lifetime commitment, and knowledge is power; the more you learn, the more valuable you become. Once you realise this, you can manage your expectations more realistically.

I recall when I was at university, I studied to ensure I passed my examinations. It was more or less a mandatory obligation, if you know what I mean. Now life has happened. I sometimes wish I had more time to read more books. Thanks to the people who invented audio and eBook's, it makes it slightly easier, but I still love my paper books, too. Call me old school if you like.

Jim Rohn said, "Formal education will make you a living and self-education will make you a fortune." If truth be told, self-education is sometimes underrated. There is no doubt that formal education is invaluable, but what you choose to learn along the way is just as important.

> **From the books you read to your daily engagements, bear in mind that learning is a lifetime commitment. Seize every opportunity you have to learn.**

RESULTS OCCUR OVERTIME NOT OVERNIGHT. KEEP GOING!

You can never build an empire if you're not surrounded by people that have an empire in their mind.

Every coach needs a coach.

MENTORSHIP AND WHY IT MATTERS

Ken Blanchard once said, "There's a difference between interest and commitment. When you're interested in doing something, you do it only when it is convenient. When you're committed to something, you accept no excuses—only results."

This is where a mentor can prove invaluable. He or she can help you to commit to your goals and vision, placing them front and centre, and accepting nothing less than the result you desire. Of course, the caveat is that you must pick a good mentor!

I am passionate about mentorship mainly because I experienced its true value. I have had the opportunity to be a mentor and a mentee, and participating in these relationships has given me opportunities to grow and contribute to the growth of others.

What exactly is mentorship? Mentorship is simply when someone who has more experience than you in a certain subject or field guides you on that subject, assisting or ensuring your progress. As you can imagine, it is easier to take someone on a journey you have already experienced.

You can decide to have a mentor for a range of things you are interested in. For example, I have career mentors, and I have a property portfolio mentor.

Having a mentor has several benefits:
- It promotes accountability.
- It exposes you to real-world experiences.
- It encourages and pushes you to be a better version of yourself.
- Mentors help you to accomplish your goals.

- Mentors are usually happy to answer questions.

The relationship between mentor (experienced adviser) to mentee (person being mentored) allows you to learn from the mistakes of others, as opposed to making the mistakes yourself. Simply put, having a mentor provides you with access to valuable information and real-world experience. Sometimes you will be required to pay for mentorship. Trust me, though, it is worth it.

> **Mentorship gives you the opportunity to choose a role model and ask questions that will help you achieve your goals.**

The concept of mentorship is a two-way street. You can be a mentor to someone else while having your own mentor, too. As I know from experience, having people look up to you indirectly also pushes you to become a better person. Both the mentor and the mentee are expected to benefit from the relationship. In other words, it is a win-win situation.

Following are some useful tips to consider when looking for a mentor. The person should have at least some of the following qualities:
- Direct or indirect experience in your desired field of interest
- Accessibility and time
- A willingness to share his or her experience with you
- A genuine desire to add value to the lives of others
- Commitment to continuous improvement, ensuring there is always something to learn
- An ability to demonstrate progress, no matter how small

A lot of successful people talk about the importance of mentorship, so there must be something about it that works. Most successful people I know or have read about have mentors. What else are you waiting for to get one?

I believe mentorship should be a lifetime commitment. The same way you eat food to ensure you are not physically hungry is the same way you should constantly feed your mind with valuable information. One of the simple ways to do so is to get a mentor.

Sarah Adenaike

I recall from my college days that I used to enjoy leadership roles, from being a student mentor to being a class representative. Surprisingly, I never quite knew I had some leadership traits in me until a later stage in my life, when one of my lecturers looked at me and said, "You are such a great leader," after assessing my performance on leadership tasks assigned to me.

I also remember an interview for an analyst position that I was pretty excited about. I had to go through stages of interview only for the interviewers to conclude I was a better fit for a leadership position. As a result, they advised me to look out for such roles on their website and apply accordingly when the opportunity presented itself. It is as though this situation brought what should have been obvious to my attention.

Being accountable to someone else forces you to leave your comfort zone; in other words, it helps you grow. I believe there is greatness in everyone, but sometimes it takes someone else to identify it in you.

You lose nothing, supporting another.

THE IMPORTANCE OF NETWORKING

Networking is an interesting topic to me personally. I wish I understood its true value a lot earlier in life. I tend to get on with people very easily, but for a very long time, I did not understand the value of maintaining some of those relationships. It's one thing to be friendly, and it's another thing to network. Networking, in simply terms, is connecting with others and developing social and professional contacts. In other words, it's not just sufficient to swap contacts; there is a level of follow-up required.

Robert Kiyosaki said in one of his famous quotes, "The richest people in the world look for and build networks, everyone else looks for work." This succinctly encapsulates the importance of networking.

I have learnt that networking is a critical part of our journeys, regardless of who or what we desire to become in life. Networking is not about who you know. Rather, it is about who knows you.

> **It is commonly said that "Your network determines your net worth," and this is no exaggeration.**

We live in a society that values your network and not just qualifications or experience. This is not to suggest that experience and qualifications are not invaluable, but your network can take you that crucial step further.

Having a good network can make your journey easier, especially where your career is concerned. I know people who by their networks have easily secured multiple opportunities.

Networking has many benefits. It increases your contact database, promotes your brand, helps with career progression, and is a form of learning in itself. It is interesting how much information I have learnt from just networking with others. Indeed, no one is an island of knowledge.

So How Does One Go about Networking?

There is no one correct way to network. Some people prefer meeting over coffee, while others prefer lunches, so be flexible in your networking approach. Bear in mind that networking does not equate to selling; this is a common misperception. View networking as just another way to create a web of contacts.

How Do I Start?

Draw a list of people you would like to network with, and find their contact details.

Choose a convenient means to initiate contact (phone or email), and then decide how to follow up. It gets easier with practice.

If you do not have a list, take advantage of networking opportunities/events, or create one yourself. Sometimes you need to come out of your comfort zone to identify your capabilities.

You can lose £50 and get it *BACK* but you can't lose 50hrs and get it *BACK* #FOCUS ON WHAT'S IMPORTANT

MANAGE YOUR FINANCES, OR THEY WILL MANAGE YOU

If you do not manage your finances, your finances will manage you. When I was at university, I didn't fully appreciate how important a lesson this is. As you can imagine, I learned quickly!

If you live, for example, in Europe, the United States, or the United Kingdom, where one can buy almost anything on credit—from a shirt to a yacht—you will understand and appreciate the value of maintaining a good credit record/score.

What Is a Credit Score?

A credit score is a numerical calculation of one's creditworthiness. This considers one's credit, debts, and defaults (failure to meet a financial obligation), if applicable. To maintain a good credit score, you must manage your finances responsibly by living within your means at the very least and ensuring your bills are paid in a timely manner.

Good Credit vs. Bad Credit Score

A good credit score is very beneficial. For example, you can get access to the best interest rates on mortgages, insurance, credit cards, and so much more. On the other hand, a bad credit score limits the options you are presented with because lenders perceive you to be a higher risk in terms of their products (for example, loans or mortgages).

Different factors can contribute to a bad credit score, including a default or late payment of bills.

Effects of a bad credit score include the following:
- Fewer employment options. For example, there are jobs in the financial sector that require a candidate to have a good credit score, along with other requirements.
- Minimised borrowing options. For example, obtaining a mortgage could be difficult if lenders perceive you as high risk. Even if you are lucky enough to be offered a mortgage, the interest rate might be higher.

> **A bad credit score does not mean you are a bad person, but unfortunately, it creates a negative impression that can have detrimental consequences where your finances are concerned.**

How Do I Avoid a Bad Credit Score?

To avoid a bad credit score, consider the following (please note that this is not an exhaustive list):
- Pay your bills promptly. This sounds like obvious advice, but you would be stunned by how complacent some people can be about bill payments.
- Never ignore letters from your creditors, and take their warning letters seriously to avoid defaulting. To put this point into perspective, if a repayment default is registered against your name in the United Kingdom, it stays on your profile for six years. Imagine the things you could achieve in six years, and then imagine how you would feel if you were, for example, declined a job opportunity based on a poor credit score. This can be frustrating to say the least.
- Open a line of communication with your creditor or creditors. If your circumstances change and are unable to meet your repayment schedule, communicate with your creditors. Explore the alternatives they offer. Most will offer a repayment plan suited to your circumstances. If you are not offered a suitable plan, ask your creditor about the plans they do offer. You'll never know what you can get if you don't ask.

- If you are in debt and need free advice, the national debt line is a good starting point. Visit https://www.nationaldebtline.org/ for more information.
- Avoid living beyond your means. Again, this may sound obvious, but a surprising number of people fall into this trap.
- Establish multiple streams of income. In other words, try not to rely on one source of income.
- Always plan your expenses within the limits of your income.
- Stay on top of your credit record by regularly checking your credit file. If you reside in the United Kingdom, the following links are helpful for checking your credit report. (There is usually a small charge with Experian and Equifax, however Noddle offers a free service.)
    - http://www.experian.co.uk/
    - https://www.equifax.co.uk/
    - https://www.noddle.co.uk/

Time out is a necessity, not a luxury.

TIME OUT

What Is Time Out?

Time out is basically time set apart to take a break from an event or circumstance. This can be done alone or with others. Many people mistakenly believe that time out is time wasted. Nothing could be further from the truth.

Life does not wait for anyone; it keeps happening whether or not you are ready. There will be occasions in life when your motivation dips, and your goals seem unobtainable. Or you're stressed because everything is not working according to plan. This is a clear signal that you need time out. At this point, many people will quit, but others will realise that time out will put them back on the path to success.

Living life with purpose and structure certainly helps you accomplish your goals and become the best possible version of yourself. But it is also necessary to plan some downtime.

> Many successful people have realised that time out is a necessity, not a luxury.

I conducted a survey with some of my previous colleagues, and 80 per cent of them revealed that they take time out for emergencies, including medical reasons, but a sizeable 20 per cent stated that time out is part of their regular routines. These people appreciate that time out helps you to recharge and refresh, and this can increase your productivity.

Time out options can include the following:
- holiday
- spa weekend
- hanging out with family and friends
- spending time alone

Potenial zone is outside the comfort zone

WALK THE WALK, DON'T JUST TALK THE TALK

The absence of confidence is one of the main reasons many people do not reach their full potentials. When you lose your confidence, you lose your voice, and when you don't have a voice, it is hard to feel your value. Life is not always easy, and sometimes nerves will triumph. But the sooner you deal with these issues, the better.

> **Sometimes you are going to have to do things regardless of your fear.**

One way to overcome fear is to challenge yourself to move out of your comfort zone and explore and do things you've never done before.

Feedback is also a very helpful tool. If you are unsure of your performance in any field or situation, try asking others for their genuine feedback, so you can understand which areas require improvement. This might sound cliché, but remember sometimes you must "fake it to make it", meaning that sometimes you must act as if you are confident to eventually become confident.

To some people, confidence comes naturally, but for others, practice makes perfect. I recommend watching *TED Talks* online as a good starting point, especially if you want to enhance your communication skills. I also recommend joining Toastmasters, although your ability to do this will vary by your location.

Here are some links to help you get started:
https://www.ted.com/talks
https://www.toastmasters.org/

Sometimes people will tell you can't because they know you can. Focus!

Don't allow the negative projection of others become your reality.

THE IMPORTANCE OF SELF-ESTEEM

What exactly is self-esteem? Self-esteem can be defined as your internal opinion of yourself; it should not be confused with confidence. For example, you can be outwardly confident and still have low self-esteem. Confidence can manifest in an ability you possess. Perhaps you are a confident singer onstage because you recognise you have a good voice, but when it comes to the person you see in the mirror, you may still feel worthless.

Different factors can contribute to low self-esteem, including having a difficult upbringing, having abusive parents, being in an abusive relationship, being around people who take you for granted, or feeling unattractive.

The opinions of others also play a significant role. In the words of Harvey Mackay, "Most fears of rejection rest on the desire for approval from other people. Don't base your self-esteem on their opinions."

> **Everyone is entitled to an opinion, but do not let the opinions of others define or shape you.**

Sadly, sometimes people voice negative opinions just to bring others down. As humans, we tend to dwell on what someone else thinks or says about us, and this can have damaging consequences.

I am unable to count the number of times I have heard people say, "They said I am not smart," or, "They said I do not qualify because I am not good enough." Too many people spend too much time ruminating about the opinions of others, especially when they are negative.

As an example, I will use the case study of someone I had the privilege of interviewing while writing this book. For obvious reasons, I will not disclose the person's real name.

Sam grew up believing he could never become significant in life, primarily because when he was a child and did something his dad considered undesirable, his dad first scolded him and then constantly told Sam he would never achieve anything significant. Over time, this adversely impacted the way Sam viewed himself. A full fifteen years later, Sam still deals with the damage caused by his dad. Whether intentional or not does not diminish the negative impact this damage has caused. The good news is that Sam is now getting help through counselling. Always remember that what we say to others has the ability to break or make them.

Another important point to remember is that you should not allow yourself to be the reason someone else's self-esteem lessens. This does not mean that you will always have something positive to say about others. Instead, it means that if for any reason you have negative feedback for someone, convey the message with wisdom and sensitivity. Unsurprisingly, thinking before speaking is a recipe that works. Or more importantly, speak to others in a way that you would like to be spoken to.

If you feel low self-esteem is an issue for you, it is important and okay to get help.

Consider the following:
- Get professional help. Google is your friend! You can look for a counsellor in your location, or explore the option of free counselling if this is available in your area.
- Challenge yourself to feel better. You can treat yourself, or do whatever you think might boost your self-esteem. Different things work for different people, so identify what works for you.
- Surround yourself with those who value and care about you.
- Maintain a positive attitude, and focus on positive things. Positive energy is contagious.

- Read books on overcoming low self-esteem. Two good examples are *Overcoming Low Self-Esteem,* by Melanie Fennell, and *Overcoming Low Self-Esteem with Mindfulness,* by Deborah Ward.
- If you know anyone who has overcome a similar challenge, do not be afraid to ask him or her for help, tips, or recommendations.
- Confide in a friend you trust, with emphasis on the word "trust".

**LIFE IS TO
SHORT
TO BE
NOTHING
BUT HAPPY**

TIME: OUR MOST PRECIOUS GIFT

I am almost certain that you have heard people say, "I do not have enough time," "Can't the time be extended," "I will do it tomorrow," or even, "Let's postpone it." It's interesting to think that we all have the same twenty-four hours in a day, regardless of where we are in the world. Some people maximise their available time, while others struggle with time management.

Time is an asset we must never take for granted. The earlier you grasp the importance of time, the better because it takes time to achieve anything in life, whether it's writing an examination or buying a house.

> **Once you understand that time is your greatest asset, you will make the most of your time and start to live a more meaningful life.**

Understanding how important time is should automatically make you want to manage your time better. Time is a gift given to all, the wealthy and the not so wealthy. The difference is how that time is managed. This does not mean time spent on leisure is wasted. Rather, it means you should strive to maximise your time in a way that works for you.

Steve Jobs once said, "Your time is limited, so don't waste it living someone else's life." No matter what ambition, vision, or dream you have—whether it is to impact lives, make money, or simply have fun—nothing can be accomplished without time.

TO EVALUATE YOUR PROGRESS MEASURE WHERE YOU ARE NOW TO WHERE YOU USED TO BE #DON'T USE OTHERS AS YOUR YARDSTICK

GOALS AND DEADLINES

Whether or not we realise it, goal setting is an important part of everyday life. For example, planning to leave your house and go out for a meal is a goal, as is planning to seek employment. In other words, goals can be big or small. With goals, there are no limits to what you can plan to achieve, so think big!

If you struggle with goal setting, try to structure each day and include goals, even small ones, as a starting point. Set mini goals for a week, and then compare the week to a week with no structure or goals. There is a distinct possibility that you will have achieved more when you planned and set goals.

Personally, apart from my big and sometimes scary goals, I have small, daily goals that eventually form part of my larger goals. Setting smaller goals helps to break down bigger plans into steps, so they become easier to manage and achieve. For instance, if your goal is to become a hairdresser, the first step would not be to open a salon. Instead, you need to break your end goal into achievable mini goals.

For example:
- Learn the hairdressing vocation.
- Acquire knowledge about what makes a good hairdresser and what clients want when looking for a hairdresser.
- Identify people with whom the passion is shared and who are ready to work with you to achieve your goal.
- Draw up a plan detailing how you will procure the necessary equipment, employ staff, and pay salaries.

Only once all these steps—and more—have been completed can you begin to find a suitable location and eventually open the salon.

> **If you do not break your end goal into steps, the likelihood of becoming overwhelmed and giving up before you even start increases.**

I am not suggesting that you cannot have big dreams. Rather, see the intermediary steps as an achievable path to your longer-term aspirations.

To increase your chances of achieving your goals, deadlines should be attached to goal setting. For ease of understanding, let us use a pregnant woman as a case study.

The known biological cycle of a pregnant woman, from conception to delivery, is nine calendar months. Now, imagine if a woman's pregnancy had no deadline; in other words, no date for the baby to arrive. Women would be miserable, and this could potentially lead to negative consequences (miscarriages, health issues, and so on).

The same principle applies to your goals. Imagine a goal without a deadline. It could remain a goal for the rest of your life, and instead of bringing you joy, it could bring you misery. Setting a deadline gives you a target to aim for. Goal setting is also an indirect way of holding yourself accountable to your dreams and aspirations.

Once you achieve your goals, do not forget to celebrate your accomplishments. Then set new goals with new deadlines. Inevitably, this allows you to grow and succeed.

EVERYONE'S PATH IS DIFFERENT.

ENJOY YOUR JOURNEY AND STOP THE COMPARISON!

A DEGREE ALONE DOES NOT EQUAL A JOB OR A BETTER FUTURE

As you can imagine, there are many graduates in the world who have yet to maximise their full potentials. There are plenty of unemployed degree holders, too. There is no doubt that a university education is a significant and beneficial investment. But many students assume that once they have completed a degree, getting a job is easy. This is far from reality.

In many cases, employers choose experience over qualifications. This can be frustrating for a new graduate. If no one offers you a job, how do you gain the required experience?

> **It is important to remain open-minded in your job hunting, and make sure you explore alternatives.**

I am an unrepentant believer that where there is a will, there is always a way. Don't spend two years of your life filling out application forms and getting no results. Create your own opportunities!

If you manage to secure an interview but are not offered the job, ask for feedback, and work on the feedback accordingly. Feedback is very important. It is an avenue to finding out what you did well and how you can improve, although this can sometimes be subjective. Candid feedback allows you to better prepare for your next interview.

In the interim, remember to explore alternatives such as the following:

- Take on internship or volunteer work. This will depend on your individual circumstances, including location, availability, and interests.
- Consider starting your own business; you never know how far you can go unless you try. I can tell you from experience that you do not need an office to start your own business. I started my first business from home. All you need is the right mindset and determination to pursue your idea.
- Consider part-time opportunities that have minimal requirements.
- Register with recruitment agencies that cover your sector of interest, and actively follow up with calls and emails to avoid simply being added to their database of interested candidates.
- Explore recommendations from people you know who are already employed. In other words, leverage off your network. Ask a friend to ask a friend if need be. This is another example of the importance of networking.
- Consider contracting. This is a less-secure form of employment, but it is an alternative route to finding the employment you want.

You dont need to fit in to make a difference, you need to stand out.

THE WORLD IS **EVOLVING** DONT BE **STATIC.**

GET INVOLVED IN EXTRACURRICULAR ACTIVITIES

Extracurricular activities help you grow and broaden your horizons. This sort of experience is also attractive to potential employers.

> **The employment market is competitive, so always think of skills and experiences that can make you stand out from the crowd.**

Following are a few ideas you can try:
- Learn a new language.
- Learn a new skill.
- Start a blog (informal writing on a website that is updated regularly). or start a vlog (using a video to share a message with others on a website).
- Participate in charitable events.

Simply put, don't be idle!

NO ONE CAN TAKE YOU BEYOND YOUR BELIEF SYSTEM.

PRACTICE THINKING OUTSIDE THE BOX

Have you ever wondered why employers are constantly looking for creative individuals who like to do things differently? Top employers are always seeking employees who can challenge the status quo with great ideas. Therefore, practice challenging the norm and thinking outside the box—within reason, of course. Do not suddenly go off on a tangent in every discussion.

When unsure, ask questions, and resist the temptation to pretend to know everything. Benefits reduce when you have a room full of people who all have the same perspective on every topic, so learn to engage in thought-provoking conversations that challenge you. I find it fascinating to listen to views that are different than mine. Even when I think differently, I still want to understand the reasoning for someone else's opinion. This is how you learn and grow.

> **Remember, there is no such thing as a foolish question. Just ask!**

Your CV is your passport to employment.

YOUR CURRICULUM VITAE (CV)

Your CV is your passport to employment. I had the privilege of being part of a recruitment process and can state, without a shadow of doubt, that sometimes the first page of the CV can decide whether a candidate is offered an interview. The reality is that we live in a fast-paced world, and recruiters do not have the luxury of spending time reading ten-page CVs. Unless, of course, this is a prerequisite when applying for a specific job.

> **It is important to ensure that your CV is concise and reflects your experiences, interests, and achievements.**

Attention to detail is also critical. The most hilarious example I can recall was when a candidate spelt stakeholders as "steak holders". This might seem minor, but to a recruiter, this could be enough to dismiss your CV and move on to the next candidate. This may seem harsh, but the world is a competitive place, and the supply of candidates often outnumbers the available jobs.

CV writing is an art form. People now get paid to write and review CVs for others. There are many free samples of CVs in the public domain, but not all are of good quality. Remember, with CV writing, practice makes perfect.

Here are a few tips on writing a good CV:
- Go straight to the point you are making. In other words, be concise.
- Let your CV showcase your achievements, qualifications, skills, strengths, and experiences.

- Tailor your CV to the vacancy you are applying for. This does not mean fabricate your experience. It just means if you have the skills the employer requires for a vacancy, highlight them.
- Do not include your address, nationality, date of birth, or marital status on your CV unless requested.
- Get someone to proofread your CV to minimise errors. Alternatively, pay a specialist CV writer to review your CV. You can run a Google search to find any CV writers and editors in your area.
- Remember to focus on quality of information, not quantity.

Please note that some roles require more than CV submission. In some instances, an application form is part of the process. If this is the case, ensure you answer the questions carefully and to the best of your ability. You can also get a third party to proofread the application form to minimise errors.

Another requirement might be a cover letter, I haven't had to write that many, but I found several templates online helpful. One of the things I recommend with cover letters is to be yourself. Authenticity is key in letting a potential employer know more about you.

What Is a Cover Letter?

A cover letter is a straight-to-the-point letter (one page preferably) that introduces a candidate to a potential employer. It highlights why the candidate is a good fit for the position. A cover letter is usually sent along with a CV, though it is not always mandatory.

Age does not constitue a barrier to those who want to learn!

Self development is the gift that keeps on giving.

SELF-DEVELOPMENT

Self-development is the gift that keeps on giving. It is a continuous process of learning and growing, and it is a key skill to master. Self-development can help you discover hidden potential you possess in addition to enhancing your self-worth. When I think about self-development, a quote by Rick Warren comes to mind: "The moment you stop learning, you stop leading." Robert T Kiyosaki echoed this sentiment in one of his famous quotes: "The moment you stop learning, you are dying."

> **In a nutshell, self-development is the art of daily and continuous improvement.**

The world is becoming increasingly fast-paced, and whether we like it or not, learning has become fluid. Something you learn that is of relevance today might not be applicable in the near future. This underscores the importance of continuous learning.

The more you learn, the more you know. It is commonly said that "Knowledge is power." Like Brian Koslow said, "Use your free time for self development." I cannot emphasise how important this is. I am always looking for ways to better myself and add value to myself.

It is often said, "The biggest room in the world is the room for improvement." Regardless of how much you have achieved or know, you can always do better. Whatever your stage of life, push yourself to learn more, be more, and do more. In other words, never stop adding value to yourself.

Job hunting is not a tick-box exercise.

FACTORS TO CONSIDER WHEN JOB HUNTING

Before you apply for a job, it is important to understand why you want the job, how you can add value to the role, and how the role will benefit you. This should be the foundation of your job hunting, even before you consider other factors, like remuneration.

> **Remember that job hunting is not a tick-box exercise.**

Here are some helpful areas to consider when job hunting:
- Work culture. From experience, this is an imperative factor to consider when choosing employment. There is no point in earning millions in an environment that makes you feel miserable. I once read a book where a man stayed in the same role for ten years for the sole reason that the job was close to his home. The sad part of it was that he was miserable and did not enjoy his work environment. I still struggle to understand why he chose to stay. Most of your time will be spent at work, so it makes sense to find a work environment you enjoy. Do your research. Ask questions during interviews. Try to get a feel of what to expect from the prospective employer, and then assess whether it is the right opportunity for you.
- Progression opportunity. Progress is a very important factor to consider. This involves some research to understand how to progress within your desired work environment. You need to find out if there is a clear progression path within a prospective firm.
- Ongoing learning. Ask yourself if the opportunity will give you the chance to learn more.
- Remuneration. Although money is not everything, your reward should at least match your skill set and experience.

- A challenging environment. Try to find a work environment that is challenging and where you have the chance to complete tasks outside your comfort zone. A challenging environment keeps you interested and helps you to grow.
- Long-term goals. Take these into account when job hunting. There is no point in building a wealth of experience in the food industry if your desire is to work in the financial sector.

Look for opportunities and if you cannot find them, create them.

GAINING WORK EXPERIENCE

You may be able to show good grades and great skills, but sometimes a lack of experience leads an employer simply not to consider your application. It is therefore a good idea to gain experience as early as possible—even if it is volunteer experience—as this enhances your chances of being offered the job you want.

Another way to look at it is to apply the principle of short-term pain for long-term gain; it will pay off in the end. It might seem frustrating to work and not get paid, but you need to understand it is just a phase and a sacrifice that you must make to achieve your long-term goals.

> Look for opportunities, and if you cannot find them, create them.

Apply for internships and ask your working friends if they have volunteer opportunities at their places of work. Whatever situation you find yourself in, do not give up. If you believe in yourself, you are already halfway there.

You must first value yourself for others to value you.

Rejection is part of the journey, keep your eyes on the price!

DO NOT ALLOW TEMPORARY DEFEAT PREVENT YOU FROM WINNING.

Sometimes their ***disappointment* leads** to your ***appointment*!**

PERSISTENCE IS CRUCIAL

What is persistence?

Persistence is the ability to carry on a course of action against all odds. In other words, persistence is basically not giving up till you accomplish your mission.

Persistence is a skill—perhaps one of the most valuable skills you can acquire. Persistence helps you to maximise your potential every day. I cannot emphasise how important it is to be persistent, but I will illustrate the value of persistence. Most of my personal achievements are due to my persistence.

Some examples come to mind. I was lucky to be able to study law at degree level. And truth be told, I had to put my social life temporarily on hold to make the most of the opportunity. I remember thinking, *I don't ever want to rewrite an examination.* When you consider how much effort it takes to pass a law exam, I am glad that I didn't have to resit any exams. I know the reason was primarily my persistence that manifested itself in my behaviour; I attended 96 per cent of early morning lectures and studied late at night at the expense of sleep.

Another example was when I started my first business. I hardly had any funds. All I had was the idea, and people often discouraged me from pursuing my dream because they knew I could not really afford it. Persistence, however, carried me through and allowed me to establish my business with minimal funding. Persistence was the fuel that kept me going. I refused to succumb, and in the end, I made something out of nothing. My first business was a one-stop shop for events. For my first event booking, I had to hire all the necessary equipment my client needed, so I made little or no profit. But fast-forward to today, and I now own quality equipment, often hiring it out to others.

The point I'm making is that regardless of where your passion lies—be it in teaching, baking, or public speaking—never give up on your dreams just because you don't have all the ingredients to turn them into reality. It is human nature that when we fail, we tend to give up because we don't want to fail again and again. We simply get tired of trying. This is borne out by reports showing many new entrepreneurs give up in the first five years.

The truth is that sometimes you must be your own biggest fan to succeed. There will not always be someone else to offer you the support or encouragement you need. You will not always get someone to like your effort/business posts on social media. Most important, always focus on your goal—your vision—and let that fuel your persistence. Never lose sight of the bigger picture, regardless of your current circumstances.

> **Despite any failure you might experience, learn to adopt an attitude of "rise and shine", regardless of the obstacles in your path.**

Learn from your failures; they are simply opportunities to do even better. And remember that sometimes if you don't ask, you don't get.

My message is simple: persistence pays off. More than 90 per cent of my achievements have been based on my persistence. Keep going, and choose to be persistent at all times.

AS YOU PROGRESS IN LIFE'S JOURNERY, YOU START TO REALISE NOT EVERYONE IS PLEASED FOR YOUR PROGRESS.... KEEP GOING REGARDLESS

Your failure is a part of your *success story.*

THE FUTURE IS YOURS

The issues discussed in this book are real. They are hurdles I have encountered on my journey, and they are relevant to everyday life. It is my deepest desire that you have learnt a lesson or two from reading my thoughts and suggestions. But most importantly, I hope you apply these lessons to your journey. I want to hear your lessons, too. Please use the official hashtag to share your lessons learnt so far (#vision2mission). We never stop learning on this interesting journey of life.

> **Remember that learning is a continuous process.**

Seize every opportunity to learn—in your daily life, in your conversations with others, or through the books you read. Always look for opportunities to learn and grow.

NOT EVERYTHING DESERVES YOUR ATTENTION.

BE SELECTIVE WITH WHAT OCCUPIES YOUR MIND.

SOMETIMES THE CRITICISM OF ANOTHER IS A REFLECTION OF WHO THEY ARE. SOME PEOPLE FEEL GOOD BY PUTTING OTHERS DOWN #FOCUS

BE CAREFUL WHO YOU SHARE YOUR IDEAS WITH. NOT EVERYONE HAS A GOOD INTENTION!

USEFUL RESOURCES

General

www.vision2mission.com
www.studentpad.co.uk
www.lifehacker.co.uk
www.sleepyti.me
www.keepmeout.com

Credit

www.experian.co.uk
www.equifax.co.uk
www.noddle.co.uk

Research

www.researchgate.net
https://www.ons.gov.uk/

Discounts

www.myunidays.com
www.studentbeans.com
www.cards.nusextra.co.uk
www.trainline.com
www.groupon.co.uk

Sarah Adenaike

Jobs

www.vision2mission.com
www.prospects.ac.uk
www.livecareer.com

Health

www.webmd.boots.com
www.nhs.uk
www.dontpassiton.co.uk

Academic

www.citethisforme.com

ABOUT THE AUTHOR

Sarah Adenaike is an award winner by the International Compliance Association for her outstanding performance award. Sarah is a qualified Financial Crime Subject Matter expert with experience working with Tier 1 investment banks locally in the U.K and globally. In addition to supporting global efforts to minimise financial crime, her goal is to raise a community of people who are maximising their potentials. People who understand that there's enough room in the sky for everyone to fly. People who are not afraid to see others win. People who are committed to self-development. She has a passion for empowerment and mentorship and derives pleasure in being able to help others. The difficulties she encountered in her transition from formal education to the real world has led her to write this book, with the primary aim of simplifying the journey of others.

www.ingramcontent.com/pod-product-compliance
Lightning Source LLC
Chambersburg PA
CBHW021014180526
45163CB00005B/1951